Published by Creative Paperbacks
P.O. Box 227, Mankato, Minnesota 56002
Creative Paperbacks is an imprint of
The Creative Company
www.thecreativecompany.us

Design by The Design Lab
Production by Chelsey Luther
Art direction by Rita Marshall
Printed in the United States of America

Photographs by Alamy (All Canada Photos), Getty
Images (Pete Oxford, Paul Souders), iStockphoto
(photoBlueIce), Shutterstock (Ji de Wet, Dennis
Donohue, EcoPrint, fivespots, Ammit Jack),
SuperStock (Steve Bloom Images, Gerard Lacz/age
fotostock, Minden Pictures, Piumatti Sergio/Prisma)

Library of Congress Cataloging-in-Publication Data
Riggs, Kate.
Tortoises / Kate Riggs.
p. cm. — (Amazing animals)
Summary: A basic exploration of the appearance,
behavior, and habitat of tortoises, the slow-moving
shelled reptiles. Also included is a retelling of Aesop's
famous fable about the tortoise and the hare.
Includes bibliographical references and index.
ISBN 978-1-60818-350-0 (hardcover)
ISBN 978-0-89812-929-8 (pbk)
1. Testudinidae—Juvenile literature. I. Title. II. Series:
Amazing animals.

QL666.C584R54 2014
597.92'4—dc23   2013002867

First Edition
9 8 7 6 5 4 3 2 1

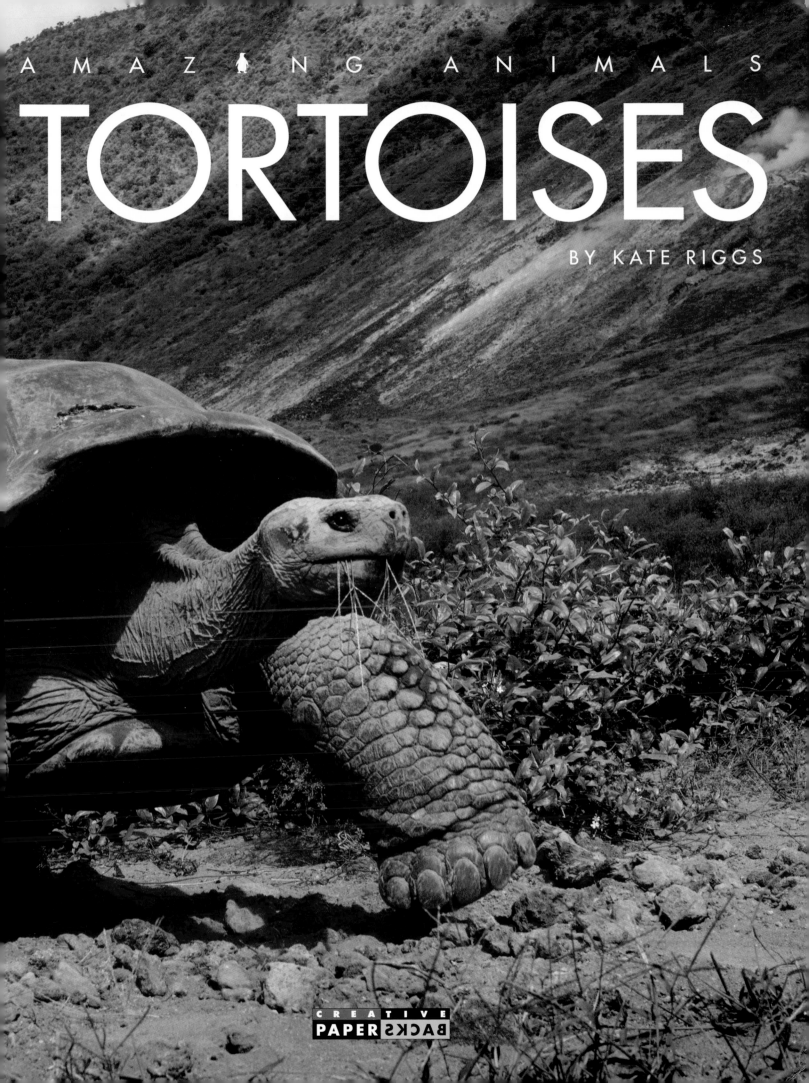

AMAZING ANIMALS

TORTOISES

BY KATE RIGGS

CREATIVE
PAPERBACKS

The leopard tortoise lives in eastern and southern Africa

A tortoise is a **reptile** that has a shell on its back. There are about 50 kinds of tortoises. Tortoises live in places that are warm and dry. Many tortoises live in Africa, India, and Southeast Asia.

reptile an animal that has scales and a body that is always as warm or as cold as the air around it

Tortoise shells are domed, or rounded. The top of the shell is hard. The bottom of the shell is softer. Tortoises move slowly because their shells are heavy.

Birds help tortoises by eating pests off their bodies

A tortoise named Lonesome George (opposite) was from the Galápagos

Some tortoises weigh as much as 500 pounds (227 kg)! Others weigh less than six ounces (170 g). That is about the weight of a hockey puck. The biggest tortoises are from the **Galápagos** (*gah-LAH-pah-gohs*) **Islands**.

Galápagos Islands a group of islands in the Pacific Ocean near the country of Ecuador

Tortoises are land animals.
They have strong legs. Tortoises use their front feet and claws to dig. They dig holes and tunnels. Female tortoises dig out nests to lay their eggs.

Desert tortoises live underground in holes called burrows

Tortoises eat many plants such as grass and flowers. They do not hunt for insects or worms. But tortoises will eat those small creatures if they find them.

Tortoises use the edges of their mouth to grab on to food

A hatchling's egg tooth falls off in a few weeks or months

A mother tortoise lays eggs in a warm nest. Three to 30 eggs **hatch** at a time. New babies are called hatchlings. Hatchlings break through their eggs using an **egg tooth**. Baby tortoises are on their own. They have to find food and take care of themselves.

egg tooth a tooth used only for breaking through the shell of an egg

hatch come out of an egg

Tortoises live alone.

They are quiet most of the time. Smaller tortoises live for 25 to 50 years in the wild. Larger tortoises can live as long as 150 years!

This tortoise lives on an island with volcanoes

Tortoises warm up in the sun. They look for food in the daytime. They sleep at night. Tortoises look for shady spots when it is too sunny.

Leopard tortoises live in grasslands where there is a lot of food

Only four kinds of tortoises live in North America. Some people go to Asia to learn about tortoises. Many people go to zoos to see big tortoises. It can take a long time for these slow reptiles to make a move!

Tortoises open their mouths and face each other when they are mad

A Tortoise Story

How can a slow tortoise win a race? A man named Aesop (*EE-sop*) told a story about this. One day, a hare, or rabbit, wanted to race a tortoise. The hare could run quickly. It knew the tortoise was slow. The hare thought it could beat the tortoise without even trying. So the hare took a nap. The tortoise kept walking and won the race!

Read More

Hatkoff, Isabella, Craig Hatkoff, and Paula Kahumbu. *Owen & Mzee: The True Story of a Remarkable Friendship*. New York: Scholastic Press, 2006.

Highfield, Andy. *Tortoises: A Beginner's Guide to Tortoise Care*. Neptune City, N.J.: T.F.H. Publications, 2009.

Websites

National Geographic Kids Creature Feature: Galápagos Tortoises
http://kids.nationalgeographic.com/kids/animals/creaturefeature/galapagos-tortoise/
This site has pictures and videos of Galápagos tortoises.

The Tortoise and the Hare Fable Crafts
http://www.first-school.ws/activities/fable/turtlehare.htm
Make finger puppets, complete a maze, or do other activities that go along with the story.

Index

digging 11
egg teeth 15
eggs 11, 15
food 12, 19
Galápagos Islands 8
habitats 4, 8, 20
life span 16
nests 11, 15
reptiles 4, 20
shells 4, 7
sizes 8
zoos 20